Let's Wonder About Science

MATTER REALLY MATTERS

J.M. Patten, Ed.D.

The Rourke Book Co., Inc.
Vero Beach, Florida 32964

PHOTO CREDITS
All photos © J.M. Patten except page 6, courtesy Alaska Center for the Environment; and page 10, courtesy Jill Parker, U.S. Fish and Wildlife Service.

Library of Congress Cataloging-in-Publication Data

Patten, J.M., 1944-
    Matter really matters / J.M. Patten.
    p. cm. — (Let's wonder about science)
    Includes index.
    ISBN 1-55916-124-8
    1. Matter—Juvenile literature. [1. Matter.] I. Title. II. Series:
Patten, J.M., 1944-   Let's wonder about science.
QC173.16.P38   1995
530.4—dc20   94-47601
                                      CIP
                                        AC

Printed in the USA

TABLE OF CONTENTS

WHAT IS SCIENCE?

When your teacher asks, "What's the matter?" that's a nice, caring question. It means, "What's wrong? Can I help you?"

Adult scientists care about you young scientists, too. However, when they talk about **matter,** they use the word in a different way. In science, matter is almost everything in the universe.

Wow, matter is important! Let's read all about it and find out why matter really matters.

Matter is all around. Water, sand and happy swimmers are all matter.

WHAT IS MATTER?

In science, matter is everything that is living—like people, plants and animals. It is also everything that is nonliving—air, water, rocks, tables, chairs and cars—even socks.

This beautiful mountain is solid matter.

The wood in this bridge is solid matter. Its properties make wood a good building material.

Matter can be big like an elephant, or tiny like grains of sand on the beach. Some kinds of matter—like you—can move around. Other kinds of matter—mountains, trees, houses, bridges—stay in one place.

Matter is fun to wonder about because all matter has **properties.** The properties of matter are easy to understand. They tell us what different kinds of matter can and cannot do.

USING PROPERTIES TO CHOOSE

Let's wonder why people choose some things and not others. Do they like the shape and color? Do they hate the taste and smell? Shape, color, taste and smell are some of the properties of matter.

People want to use rubber boots, umbrellas and raincoats on a rainy day. They have the kind of properties that help us stay dry.

To build a birdhouse, people use nails, wood, glue, saws and hammers. The properties these tools have make them good for that job. Could you build a good birdhouse if your saw were a comb and your hammer a jelly doughnut?

We choose an umbrella to keep us dry on a rainy day or in the shade on a sunny one.

USING PROPERTIES TO DESCRIBE

We can describe a bird by listing its properties. It has feathers, two wings, and it flies.

We can list the properties of a dog, too. It has four legs, soft fur, a tail, and it barks.

People describe most things by listing their properties. Properties make a dog different from a bird and a bird different from a dog.

The properties of this sea bird help it swoop quickly along the water to catch its dinner.

WHAT MAKES MATTER ALIKE?

In some ways, all matter is alike.

All matter contains some kind of "stuff" that's called **mass.**

All matter takes up space. That's called **volume.**

We can lean up against a tree, but we can't walk through it.

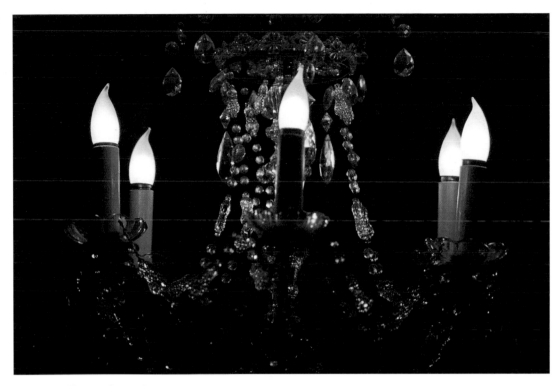

The yellow glow from the light is not matter. Light has no mass or volume.

You and your best friend have mass and volume, so you can't stand in the same space at the same time. You can try, but you'll step on each other's toes. You each take up your own special space.

A car that tries to enter the space of another causes a dented fender. Have you ever tried to enter a tree's space? It has its own special space, too.

MATTER CAN BE SOLID

Everywhere we look, we see matter. Our Earth has **solid** matter like mountains and trees.

People carry books to school, write with pencils, and eat sandwiches at lunch. All these things are solid forms of matter, too.

One way to describe a solid is to tell about its shape. Most balls are round. Snakes are long. A property of all solid matter is that it has a shape of its own.

Pumpkins have a shape of their own.

MATTER CAN BE LIQUID

Oceans, rivers, lakes and puddles are **liquid** forms of matter. Liquids can be thick—like pancake syrup—or thin and runny—like paint.

Properties help describe liquids. One property of all liquids is that they take on the shape of the container that holds them. Your glass of juice would be a puddle without the glass to hold it.

Unlike solids, liquids do not have a shape of their own. That's one way liquids are different from solids.

The water in this river is liquid matter.

MATTER CAN BE GAS

The third kind of matter is called **gas.**

The air we breathe is a gas. The steam rising from a big pot of boiling water is also a gas.

A gas called helium keeps these balloons flying high.

The steam from a teapot is a gaseous form of matter.

Gas has interesting properties. Gas will completely fill any closed container. When released, gas floats rather than spills, and spreads out in all directions.

We sometimes use a gas called **helium** to fill balloons. You have to hang on tight to that kind of balloon or it will float up out of your reach. That's an important property of helium—it rises.

WHAT'S NOT MATTER?

Let's wonder what might not be matter.

Is a shadow matter? A person can stand in your shadow. A shadow is not matter because it does not take up its own space.

Sunshine is not matter, either. It can shine on the water and feel warm on your face, but sunshine does not take up space. It is not matter.

Sound moves through the air to your ears, but takes up no space as it travels. Sound is not matter.

A shadow is not matter.
The ball sits in the shadow's space.

GLOSSARY

gas (GASS) — the form of matter without shape or volume

helium (HEE lee um) — a gas that rises

liquid (LI kwid) — the form of matter in which the molecules flow

mass (MASS) — the amount of matter in an object

matter (MAT er) — anything that has mass and takes up space

properties (PRAHP er teez) — things about matter that make it different from other kinds of matter

solid (SAH lid) — the form of matter that has its own shape

volume (VAHL yoom) — the space that matter takes up

A reflection is not matter, but the dog can still think he's handsome.

INDEX